**100 days, 100 GRAND**

"**How to do School**" first UK edition 2020

First published in Great Britain in 2020 by Redpump Ltd. Copyright © Chris Worth 2020.

This print paperback perfect bound edition 1 of "How to do School" is ISBN 978-1-912795-31-4

See 100days100grand.com

*To the late **Chuck Baldwin***

*One of life's true good guys*

*Who loved education ... and all it enabled.* 🤔

*"All kids have talents.*

*And we squander them pretty ruthlessly."*

—Sir Ken Robinson

I dropped out of school at 16, so I could start my education.

Decades later, it's far from over. But while I'm no teacher, self-educating to compete as a one-man business (with the odd year out for a "proper" degree) taught me what a young person *really* needs to thrive. (And I *have* authored a textbook*, a reasonably hard practical exercise in teaching.)

My conclusion: school has a single purpose. And schools today deliver it very, very badly. It's not to fulfil some societal goal. Or make you a good citizen. Or even tell you what 2+2 equals. (Although that helps.)

School should be about teaching kids to *think*.

Thinking is how we integrate concepts. Understand reality. Make use of information, and make sense of our world. Yet with pre-18 curricula clogged with rote-learning, over-testing, and politicised junk like "citizenship classes" and "diversity awareness", the skill of thinking is rarely developed in any school. And today's anti-intellectual trends—fake news, conspiracy theories, populism, antivaxxing—are a direct result.

So—with a debt to two short masterpieces, Leonard Peikoff's "Teaching Johnny to Think" and James Tooley's "The Beautiful Tree"—this little book reimagines schooling, and how it could work better.

Let's start the lesson.


CHRIS WORTH

* 100days100grand.com. (There, it's in.)

# WHAT THIS BOOK COVERS

In the words of legendary British educator Ken Robinson, we have to rethink the fundamental principles on which we are educating our children. This little book attempts to do so, noting the problems with (mostly State) schooling worldwide and suggesting solutions.

After defining a goal for school, it starts by listing the big issue and its contributing factors. (All five of them.) Then it explores whether schooling should be more businesslike, its critical success factors, and teacher's pay. It goes on to note what's *good* about today's school model—more than you think—and what needs to change: the school year, curriculum subjects, how school should be taught and graded. Finally, there's a funding model that supports schooling's revised goal, recognising the value it creates and rewarding who creates it.

Note that while it's about children's education, it doesn't have much to say about preschool, or even the pre-adulthood 16-18. This is about the years from 6 to 16. Because done correctly, ten good years are plenty to equip a young person with the skills needed to negotiate the $21^{st}$ century . . . and not just survive, but thrive.

First up: the one (and only) thing school absolutely must do . . . and rarely does.

# THE PRIMACY OF THINKING

The UK has 800,000 NEETs: young people not in employment, education, or training. One in nine adults has no qualifications at all; five million over-18s are functionally illiterate. In the USA, the figure is 43 million, including 13% of all 17-year-olds. Social mobility in the "land of the free" is lower than in Old Europe.

All these outcomes stem from a few critical years in life: the school years, roughly from age 6 to 16. And at the international scale, they don't correlate with wealth. The illiteracy rate of India—where hundreds of millions still lack electricity and plumbing—differs from the USA's by a single percentage point. While

China, a rising world power but with vast regions still poor, has it sussed, with adult literacy of 97%.

Of course, grades aren't everything. But literacy is a partial proxy for something more basic in a successful life: the ability to *think*.

Thinking is the one skill nobody can thrive without. Yet State schools (and plenty of private ones) do their best to *expel* thinking from the schoolday.

School, for the overwhelming majority worldwide, is a toxic wasteland of rote memorisation and standardised tests. It frustrates the smart kids, lets down the slower ones, and fails anyone *remotely* neurodiverse. And when "real" education begins—after 18, when Higher Education demands critical thinking and problem-solving—it's failing to equip people for it. (In the USA, between 40 and 60% of first-year university students take remedial literacy and numeracy classes.)

School should be a wondrous adventure, where people discover their preferred modes of learning and acquire abilities that set them up for a lifetime of self-actualised productivity. Not parroting the preferred bullshit of who Henry VIII divorced or decapitated.

School should teach *how* to think. Not *what* to think.

This means school—for the sake of argument, everything you're taught from 6 to 16—needs a total rework. Stripping education back to its essentials, and rebooting with the common denominator: **how to think**.

(Those who *can* think tend to learn the skill later on,

in Higher Ed or out in the world. In other word, in *spite* of school, not thanks to it.)

There's huge economic benefit in doing so: defined as those who've completed two years of undergrad education or equivalent, people who've learned to think show 30% greater earnings at age 40. An education to age 16 that teaches young people how to *think* is worth far more than the average MA humanities degree.

So thinking is the one thing schools absolutely need to teach.

Let's look at what's stopping them.

# THE TROUBLE WITH SCHOOL

Why *don't* schools teach kids to think?

There are five simple reasons. But a sixth lurks less obvious, dwarfing them all: they just don't want you to.

Most schools are run by the State. And the few that aren't have to follow a lot of the same rules. Meaning: the goal of schools is the goal of government. Less about teaching you to be an effective individual, more about turning you into a "good citizen".

This basic conflict underpins all that's wrong in the education sector.

Because according to government's unwritten definition, a "good citizen" isn't an individual. It's someone who sees herself as part of a tribe, who puts the State's (sorry—"other people's") interests above their own. It's someone obedient, acquiescent, *dependent*.

Governments need you to think they're vital to your life. That's how they take half your income. Dictate what you can and can't do. And get endlessly bigger.

(Great skies above, the *last* thing they want is people *thinking*! Citizens might start working out just what poor value government is. Or how few people it really represents.)

This is why you see skilled and energetic teachers leaving the profession within five years, sobbing and broken, dragged to the dirt by the system that surrounds them. It didn't let them do what they thought they were there for.

(If you're wondering how a bad system can have good people within it, check out the academic discipline called Organisational Behaviour, or OB. First thing you learn is how wildly divergent the motivations of the organisation and the individuals in it can be.)

So while it's not (really) the fault of the teachers, the appalling truth is this: **government schools fail children**. Absolutely, completely, and everywhere.

That's our first, perhaps over-dramatised problem: government schools ultimately answer a government agenda.

Let's break that agenda into parts, before we try to break the agenda itself.

# 1. Percepts vs. concepts

The most important factor in the State agenda: schools today teach *perception* not *conception*.

Put simply, it means kids are shown the *what* and not the *why*. "Learning" is based on concretes: alleged facts presented as-is, without any broader context. The Donner Party. Quadratic equations. Tudors and Stuarts. The Laws of Motion. Sutton Hoo. Course materials are essentially snapshots, torn out of reality. So children learn the route to schooling success is to rote-memorise stupefyingly dull lists and accept concretes in isolation: percepts. Not "thinking" at all.

Learning to think needs *concepts*.

Concepts are what separate the human from the

animal. Wild creatures are perceptual: their entire behaviour stems from what they see and hear and smell, a worldview of "Believe what you're looking at". If humans have a special talent, it's the ability to *question* what's there, to form abstract theories and organise reality into general models and special cases.

This ability—understanding the world through concepts—is at the core of thinking.

Yes, there's a reason for teaching school as concretes. Concepts take longer. They need engagement and interactivity between the mind of teacher and pupil; they need illustrating with a variety of examples, often ranging far from the lesson plan, before the underlying idea is understood. Yet doing so isn't optional, because conceptual understanding—the capacity to abstract ideas, to grasp common denominators in what we perceive—is what makes us human. Philosophically, it's an omission of **epistemology**, how we know things.

It's a Hard Problem to solve, especially when a teacher today will be penalised for solving it. But there's no escape: teaching children to think must start with *concepts*.

## 2. A crowded curriculum

Second factor: the school curriculum is like anything else in government, in that it accrues cruft without shedding anything that went before. (Government's success metric is about getting bigger. Not better.)

The UK's now includes 14 compulsory subjects and numerous others taught to different age groups, in a week that fits in barely 20 teachable hours. This is absurd, allowing no depth in any subject and layering on the khumbaya'ing of social justice before the basics have bedded in. And it's getting worse.

Schools introduce Gender Studies as a subject, when three in ten British school-leavers are functionally illiterate. They "teach" Sex and Relationships as if it substituted for personal experience. And let's not *start* on Citizenship Classes, or Cultural Awareness, or the other Wars and Wokery that've infested post-11 schooling these last few decades.

Whether or not you agree they're useful life skills, nobody can claim they're fundamental to thinking. Those critical early years *must* be about *fundamentals*. No building can stand without a foundation.

If the percepts vs. concepts problem is schooling's epistemology, this is its **metaphysics**, or the nature of reality: kids are learning irrelevancies before they've got a grip on the basics.

Again, none of it is about *thinking*.

# 3. Methods, not outcomes

Third up: education authorities from Japan to Germany are obsessed with process, not practice. The length and format of lessons, when to take tests, box-ticks and paper-pushing that take up 40-60% of the average UK teacher's workload before they even get to plan an actual lesson. (Much less teach it.)

There's no faster way to demotivate a trained professional than to mandate methods over outcomes. And—treated as franchisees rather than empowered experts—teachers have responded with a collective "Fuck it".

This is why the multiple-choice test has become the principal exam methodology worldwide. It's why 49%

of A-level students get straight A's, making the exam meaningless. It's why teachers spend classroom hours on exam technique, when it's obvious to all of them which kids are making hay and which are rolling in it.

What matters are *outcomes*, not methods. And the worst part of this: teachers are perfectly capable of producing them, if the tyranny of testing is taken away. Again from philosophy, this is the **politics** branch: how it should all be organised.

So school needs to focus less on the minutiae of testing, and more on *the skills kids acquire*, assessed as individuals. There's no reason for monthly tests if the outcome is a self-actualised youngster equipped to take on the world.

## 4. Division, not unity

The school day is chopped into discrete hours, with subjects in silos. Even within subjects, today's preferred method is what differs, not what unites. Trouble is, that's not how our brains work.

You learn a new thing in terms of what you already know, comparing and contrasting it to existing knowledge until it settles in as part of the whole. Learning is a process of integration.

In fact, the whole of *consciousness* is an ongoing process of integration and differentiation. Connecting thoughts, collecting them into networks, separating them into different schema. Maths and physics are not separate; the former is a tool for exploring the latter.

Writing is not a subject; it's a discovery method that connects all the others. Even PE isn't a discrete hour on Wednesdays and Fridays; it's a tool that builds a healthy connection between mind and body.

Rote learning is perhaps the worst example of subject siloism. For many kids it fosters a lifelong *dislike* of learning. (By contrast, the IB—International Baccalaureate—makes a decent fist, presenting its six subjects as a connected whole. But it's rarely offered in State schools.)

The philosophical branch here is **logic**: how we apply reason. A rounded education is a body of interlinked knowledge, each schema made more effective by those around it. School needs to connect.

## 5. Serving the wrong customer

Fifth and last brings us full circle. In any situation where your customer isn't who you think it is, the incentives to *serve* that customer are distorted.

With schools, the customer should be plain: kids and parents. But a State school's real "customer" is government. It's government who sets standards, carries out inspections, decides whether or not the school can even exist. You don't mess with the money.

Yes, the basic problem with state schools is the same as with the whole of public service. (An issue of **ethics**, how we decide the right thing to do.)

It's why everywhere in the world, State school is a soul-deadening, creativity-destroying, life-denying place. And why almost any *private* school is a happier, more stimulating, and more effective one. Because a private school's interests are aligned with the right customer: the parent paying the fees.

Of course, State schools have one advantage over private ones: they're free. Or at least, not sending invoices to parents each term. But as we'll see later, there are ways the State sector can align incentives the way the private sector does, without total costs to the taxpayer changing.

So: satisfying customers, serving markets, aligned incentives. That sounds a lot like a "business", doesn't it?

Let's ask that question, next.

# IS EDUCATION A BUSINESS?

Bureaucrats categorise UK education on nine levels. There's a 0 (sorry, "entry level") for those without experience or qualifications of any kind. Levels 1-3 cover British GCSEs and A-levels / NVQ 1-3 and Ordinary National Certificates/diplomas, equivalent to American K-12. Level 4 is undergrad study or a skilled trade (K-14) and so on up. While the names of individual qualifications can sound confusing, the model provides a logical sequence through degrees and their vocational equivalents, all the way to Level 8 (PhDs and postdocs).

Here's the key: the level you reach correlates with the value you add to the economy. Which, in a free market, is a good proxy for what you earn.

And it's *exponential*. Returns kick in at Level 4 and get more pronounced as you climb the ladder, with the average graduate showing a lifetime earnings uplift of over £100,000 and the top 10% (around half of those with a Master's degree) over £500,000.

(Note these are "present value discounted" figures, with an allowance made for the lower value today of income further off. Without discounting they'd be dramatically higher. Well, except for the non-degrees fooling some students into thinking there's an easy option . . . but *you* didn't do those, did you?)

So while there's argument around the edges, the conclusion is clear: *education pays*. At least if you keep at it until you're 20. Higher Education provides a professional service, charging fees that reflect value delivered. Which, in a free market, is the definition of a business.

But does that make *children's* education a business?

Yes. Because education is *cumulative*.

If you're functionally illiterate at 14, the probability you'll make it up later is almost zero. The years from 6-16 are absolutely critical; statistically, a 17-year old NEET is a write-off. You may as well strangle him in his sleep and save a lifetime of welfare claims.

(Just kidding. You knew that, right?)

So those years to 16 are the Great Enabler, setting a child up for a lifetime of productive outcomes. This is a service worth paying for. Ask South Korea, whose evening cram schools have turned a developing nation into one of the most advanced in barely a generation. Or China, whose pushy parents have led to 5%+ GDP growth for decades on end. Or Japan post-1950. Or Singapore since the 60s. Or . . .

Enough. School is a business, so our model will treat it as such. Starting with working out what products and services will actually satisfy customers and succeed in the market.

But before that, let's work out what makes school *work*.

# TEACHERS: the factor that matters

In the West, the common view of teachers is that they're a bunch of union-obsessed, anti-meritocratic, capitalist-bashing Marxists with a trendily Woke view of history, who love Big Government as much as their long holidays and index-linked pensions.

All of which is true.

It's just not the whole picture.

Most teachers genuinely love the job—at least the part of it that involves actual teaching. Which, sadly, is a tiny fraction of what teachers are asked to do.

In the UK, a teacher's social life is a Soviet-era whirl of mandated meetings, guidelines to follow, tests to mark and boxes to tick. There are evenings to attend, assessments to oversee, conferences and programmes to plan for.

But ask any of them whether they'd rather be in the classroom, teaching, and 80%+ will say Yes.

Teaching is *hard*. It's one of the caring professions. It takes skill, resolve, and energy, and the number of people who can do it well is small. As with management skill in business, no more than 1 in 20 people are capable of teaching, and probably fewer.

Yet a good one can do extraordinary things. Like set a flatlining childhood on course for a lifetime of success, in just a few hours a week.

And that's why the biggest—perhaps the *only*—factor that matters in children's education is **the teacher**.

Not buildings. Not class size. Not playing field acreage. *Teachers*.

A building with modern classrooms, multimedia studios, science labs and football fields isn't a "school" if there are no teachers there.

But the meanest backstreet hovel can be a school, if there's a teacher in it.

Across Asia and Africa's poorest neighbourhoods, you'll see signs for private institutions offering alternatives to the State. They're not in great buildings. (Many are near-derelict.) They're not staffed by noted academics. (Few have degrees.) But they're great *schools*, simply because they have to be. Those that don't provide value (and poor parents want value above all) don't stay open long.

The best physics teacher isn't one with a PhD. It's an engaged person who enjoys science, with a genuine love of imparting knowledge.

So now we know the problems, here's the start of our solution. If we want schools that teach children how to think, we'll only get them by putting teachers front and centre. Engaging them. Enabling them. Empowering them.

Good teachers are the only factor that counts in child education. NOTHING ELSE MATTERS.

Write that in two-metre letters on the wall of every school in the world.

## TEACHERS' PAY

Now we've established the core of schooling is the teacher, let's talk about teaching pay. Taking our British example:

==The starting salary for a teacher should be £53,000==, rising to £165,000 for sustained success over decades in the game.

That's a lot higher, at both outset and endgame, than British teaching salaries today. (And yes, we're going to back it up in the financial model later.) The reason is simple:

In a free market, you are paid according to the difficulty of the problem you solve. And educating youngsters is *extremely* difficult.

95% of jobs aren't like that. The man mopping floors or picking potatoes is doing a vital job, yes. He's working hard. But it's not a *difficult* job. It's a job anyone could do.

So if we're treating children's education the way we should—as a business, where skilled professionals deliver value-added outcomes in a competitive economy—teachers deserve a piece of the action.

That's where our £53,000 comes from: it's the 96th percentile of British salaries. The point where real benefits to GDP kick in: the people not just "doing the job", but doing it better than the next guy.

(Sorry, recent graduates: you won't earn that at 22. You'll have to prove yourself first, like any junior doctor or banker. But in our model, once you do that—

say, after three years in the saddle—the gold starts rolling in. And let's face it: a salary scale that hits six figures in five years would attract a *lot* of applicants.)

So this book proposes high teaching pay as a given—a "market rate"—and works back to a financial plan where it fits. (Which, if we take a big-picture view, turns out to be easier than you think.)

No question, teaching should be a high-paid profession. If we make it one, all the problems of unionised bargaining, bad teachers staying in post, and strike threats go away. (There's a reason high-paid people rarely belong to unions.)

Let's look for that model. But before that, a few conditions.

# THE AGE OF LEARNING

This book sets 6 as the age school starts. A bit later than most countries. (Although the same as Finland, whose State system is among the most lauded.) Which will have many pushy parents out on the streets in protest.

There are options for pre-6 education. The one that works is Montessori. But it's expensive, and largely closed to the low-waged. So: what should kids be doing before they reach school age?

How about "being kids"?

The trouble with much "preschool" is that it's like school. You'll see desks, books, blackboards, toddlers strapped in for a joyless commute to adulthood. What nonsense. Kids need to be *kids*.

An early joy of learning comes from playing, discovering, getting scabs on their knees and crayons up their noses. When we deny this, chaos rules. 25% of America's school-age children are on prescription drugs, largely to make them behave in a way the school requires. (Take a guess how many of these medicated children no longer have problems when they're educated with more understanding.)

It's the same at the other end of childhood. While most school systems run into the adult era, graduating them at 18, there's little point in two extra years when school hasn't worked for the first 10. So let's treat school as what happens from 6 to 16—not 5 to 18.

Accordingly, this little book, with a focus on

teaching children to *think* rather than *remember*, treats child education as a ten-year journey. Less than many State systems. But with a much narrower curriculum focussed on a single goal, a decade is all you need.

And if you agree kids should play until 6 and forget further decisions until 16, those ten years can give them all *they'll* ever need.

## THE MORE THINGS CHANGE...

Amid this negativity, a side note: not *everything* about school needs to change. In fact, in the model this book proposes, a lot of the "hardware" of schooling is unchanged.

The model of school being a building kids attend for a set number of hours each day remains a good one. It provides structure, allows planning, socialises kids and keeps parents passably sane. (Although the school day and year need to change, big time.) So let's keep the buildings.

Nor does it mean changing the basic way lessons are delivered. With the right approach to instruction and group work, the sage-on-a-stage in front of a whiteboard *works*. Teaching to think doesn't need a change in the skill of teaching itself. So conventional pedagogy remains in play, too.

And whizzy new technology isn't a panacea, either. There's a huge role for Zoom, WhatsApp, mobile communications, and online resources like Khan Academy and DuoLingo to assist teachers—but tech is a tool in the box, nothing more. (With technology moving so fast, adopting any platform as a longterm teaching theatre carries risks.) The peoply stuff of a competent professional instructing a class in person still works.

There are many things that must change. But these things should stay the same.

## (THE SCHOOL IN THE HOME)

*Another* side note: homeschooling.

Oh dear. Oh dear. Oh dear.

You'd think homeschooling would be a viable option for parents dissatisfied with the State system. And while different countries accept it to different degrees (the USA fairly tolerant, the UK less so) it's at least possible in most nations.

Trouble is, "homeschooling" has an Ewww-factor. Deservedly so. Because a great deal of it is faith-based.

As the opposite of reason, religion is precisely what you *don't* want at school. It is actively in opposition to the goal of teaching children to think.

(What do the world's religions want you to do above all? Obey, *without* thinking. They're a bit like governments, tbh.)

To test this, look at any selection of "homeschooling materials" from the mostly-American organisations offering materials.

They are universally appalling.

Which means any homeschooler wanting to give their kids a *real* education needs to get creative. Fortunately, there *are* thousands of resources . . . from *non*-homeschooling organisations. Your decisions will be guided by what to leave out, not what to include. khanacademy.org, duolingo.com, youtube.com: free lectures and study materials abound.

So any competent parent *can* put together a

homeschooling programme that teaches reading, writing, languages, a love of literature, resolves math anxiety, and imparts a genuine love of learning. That develops healthy attitudes to food and exercise. Teaches how to build arguments through objectivity and reason. With, even, the chance of social interaction with likeminded peers.

The proviso: there aren't many of you, and you're going to have to devote large volumes of time and energy to homeschooling your child.

And if you're not a teacher yourself, it'll be harder.

So with that, it's time to propose our model for school.

# A MODEST PROPOSAL

So we know what we'll keep. And we know what doesn't work. Our next question: what *does*?

Our proposal for changing the nature and purpose of school starts with some changes to school hours. It continues with what school should and shouldn't teach, with a few surprises. Finally, it proposes actual curriculum subjects.

Above all, though, it's a change in **grading** that matters: a paradigm shift in how work is *assessed*. Our proposed change is big in scope, different in approach, doesn't scale well, and only teachers can do it.

That's fair. Teaching isn't supposed to be easy.

# Changes to the school day

The schoolday should coincide with the workday of parents. After all, it used to.

Before the Industrial Revolution, most people worked in fields. So school (such as it was) opened at daybreak, closed mid-afternoon, and shut entirely over Summer as students exchanged school for scythe.

Today, most parents work from around 9 to around 5, year round. So should school.

The proposal: schools open from 8am to 6pm with a one-hour lunchbreak, like most offices. Lessons start at 9. Two 90-minute sessions in the morning. Two more in the afternoon. Six contact hours per day. *Maybe* a half day on Fridays.

If that sounds like a lot, our model suggests plenty of guided discovery outside formal lessons. "Being taught" will cover perhaps half those hours. But learning to *think* will span all of them.

That's all.

## Changes to the school year

Also in need of change is the traditional school year of three terms with a long summer break.

A longer school day allows more learning. But with schooldays from 6 to 16 rather than 5 to 18, there are fewer days on the docket. So let's say school is open fulltime, but kids get two weeks off in every two months with no lessons. (They can still go in.)

Who sets when that fortnight off happens? Simple: the school does.

There's no reason every school in the land should shut in July and open again in September. Indeed, it's a very bad idea. 2020's pandemic, which led to British schools closing for up to six months, arguably led to a full year of schooling forgotten by an entire cohort.

So, a workable model: six weeks on, two weeks off. Year round.

With a bonus for parents: without the demand spike in July and August, family holidays will get a lot cheaper.

# TEN THOUSAND HOURS

So: 30 contact hours each week. Six weeks of every two months in class. A total of 1,080 contact hours per year. Call it a round 1,000, for ten years from age 6-16.

==Ten thousand hours to equip a child for a successful life==.

That's enough. *Way* enough.

In ten thousand hours, you can become an expert in anything. And that includes thinking.

## WHAT SCHOOL SHOULD TEACH ...

So now we've got a workable education model, what and how should schools actually *teach*?

The answer: a ==minimalist and interconnected curriculum that develops the ability to think above all==. Delivered in a way that lets each child develop a learning modality that works for them, on the way to becoming a self-actualised adult.

Sounds avant-garde?

This is the darkly comic core of all that's wrong with schooling today: it's actually the oldest model of education known.

When Plato hung out his shingle in 387BCE, his academy offered just six subjects. Over in Asia, the forebears and disciples of Confucius (孔夫子) had already been doing the "Six Arts" for centuries. Mesopotamia and Egypt, earlier still, managed with five. The Western concept of the Renaissance Man came millennia later, yet intellectual life prospered with (arguably) a *single* subject: the study of Latin classics.

What unites all these approaches: a curriculum that was *limited*, yet *canonical*. The minimum necessary, but no less, resulting in a fully educated individual capable of meaningful action.

It meant focussing on the basics: reading, writing, mathematics. (We'll forget the archery and chariot stuff for now.) Each learned at a higher level each year, and intellectually unified in a way that made the sum greater than the parts.

An early focus on Latin grammar led wealthy Europeans first to history, with Caesar's Commentaries. Then mathematics and science, with Euclid and Pliny, then (sadly) god stuff, with Jerome's bash at the Bible. Later came moral choices, with Ovid. If you spoke Latin, you'd learned to think.

Learning to think doesn't need a lot of subjects. It just needs a lot of *connected concepts*.

That's why our model for modern education is minimal—just three subject areas. But even more important is the "basics". Because they permeate everything, as Latin permeated Renaissance Europe.

So: basics first.

# THE NEW SIX ARTS

Five of the six basics in our model—not so much subjects as modalities—are familiar to any teacher today: **reading, writing, listening, speaking**, and **arithmetic**. With one that isn't: **logic**.

What's different in our approach is the way we use them. They're not separate subjects leading to certificates. There's no English Composition GCSE in our model. RWLSAL are ways of approaching and understanding all *other* subjects, methods for thinking taught and reinforced in every lesson.

Here they are, one by one.

# Reading, and the book

Fortunately, plenty of schools still use the right method to teach reading in the earliest years: synthetic phonics. It's right because it's *conceptual*.

The "concept" of k, p, t and z representing sounds is taught with examples; the child unifies that small set into a coherent system for reading almost anything. That's the great thing about concepts: they reveal the simplicity and unity beneath surface complexity.

Some educators object to phonics because it's "artificial". But that's precisely its point. It engages key attributes of thinking, like selective attention and model-building. (Compare this to the still-in-use 1970s-era "look-say" method, which is entirely concrete . . . and entirely useless.) That's the beauty of a conceptual approach: once a concept is internalised, its general applicability makes it powerful.

But "reading" is more than sounding out words. That's why beyond the early years, the primary learning method across all subjects must be **the book**. *Actual* books, big white papery things with a distinct topic, sequence of chapters, contents page, and index. Because exploring a text to build mental models and find answers is a core skill of thinking.

Books are conceptual, too. A book *binds* knowledge together. (No prizes for guessing where *that* verb came from.) Reading is the gateway to the conceptual world: you can't read *without* thinking.

Virtual books are fine, and may be the only option

for some schools. But the best book becomes its owner's property, to scribble in, dogear, add value to. *That's* a book.

So no taking the textbook away from a child at year's end. The ideal textbook is a multi-year project.

In our model, a child learns to think principally by reading books, with the teacher's role to guide and check understanding. Along with the other most basic skill of all: **writing**.

# Writing, and the essay

Of the four basic communication skills—reading, writing, listening, and speaking—by far the most important in learning to think is writing.

So writing is *not* limited to what's taught in English lessons. It's the basic skill of organising concepts into understandable form.

You understand a topic best when you have to explain it to others at a distance. And writing—deciding an approach, planning a structure, constructing and revising sentences and paragraphs in logical sequence—is how you do that. (Even if it's going to be delivered as spoken word.)

Of course, reading is a prereq. But with that done,

writing is how a student best explores a topic and embeds it in learned experience. It's how someone learns to make *use* of what they've absorbed.

To teach kids to think, first teach them to write.

All school subjects should be assessed principally by a method that goes back to ancient China's civil service exams: **the written essay**. A short but complete text that invokes the skill of thinking. Not multiple choice tests. Because you can't wing it with an essay; a blank sheet of paper gives you nowhere to hide. (At the school level, teachers are uncanny detectors of bullshit. Unlike college professors, who are generally purveyors of it.)

Of course, this takes more teaching time. But that's the point of adopting writing as a *modality*, not a *subject*. It maximises contact hours and minimises box-ticking. Pass or fail is left to the person best placed to judge it: the teacher who knows the student as an individual.

Last, separate writing from "handwriting". Writing by hand is getting less valuable by the year. Post early years, let them use keyboards, by all means; some skills aren't worth the time. (If that sounds too much, remember writing itself worried the ancient Greeks, who thought it'd kill the talent of memorising epic poems. It did. But does anyone value *that* skill today?)

Our model treats writing is the basis of learning for all subjects, assessed by the essay. Next: **listening**.

# Listening, and the lesson

We had the book as the core of reading. The essay as the core of writing. The core of listening is the **lesson**.

"Sage on a stage", with a lesson plan featuring an opening gambit, teaching material, and conclusions, plus questions and class discussion to check understanding, remains the basis of effective learning for the huge majority of kids. Which means developing the ability to *listen*.

So far, so standard. What's different is that in our model, listening is a much more deeply taught skill, with exercises and assessments.

(It's a normal way of teaching non-native languages. Why is it so rare in native?)

The bonus here is that teaching listening as a skill restores something arguably lost in today's soundbite world, where interruption and volume are the tools rather than reasoned response. The thinking person is someone capable of understanding what someone says before responding. It's a civilised way to behave, too.

In today's YouTube and TikTok'd world, kids are arguably better at listening than their parents. So let's use it. And this is where schools don't need to change much. Everyone likes to be listened to.

# Speaking, and the presentation

The ancient Greeks put great store in the skill of using language to persuade, as the art of **rhetoric**. It wasn't speechifying; rhetoric was a triangle involving the *ethos* (presenter) *pathos* (audience) and *logos* (context). Only with attention to all three would a presentation be successful.

In schools today, presenting to an audience is more special occasion than everyday occurrence. That's sad, because speaking to an audience is among the best ways to hone clarity of thought.

That's why speaking is another of our basic six skills used in every subject, with its main tool the **oral presentation**. An essay in spoken form.

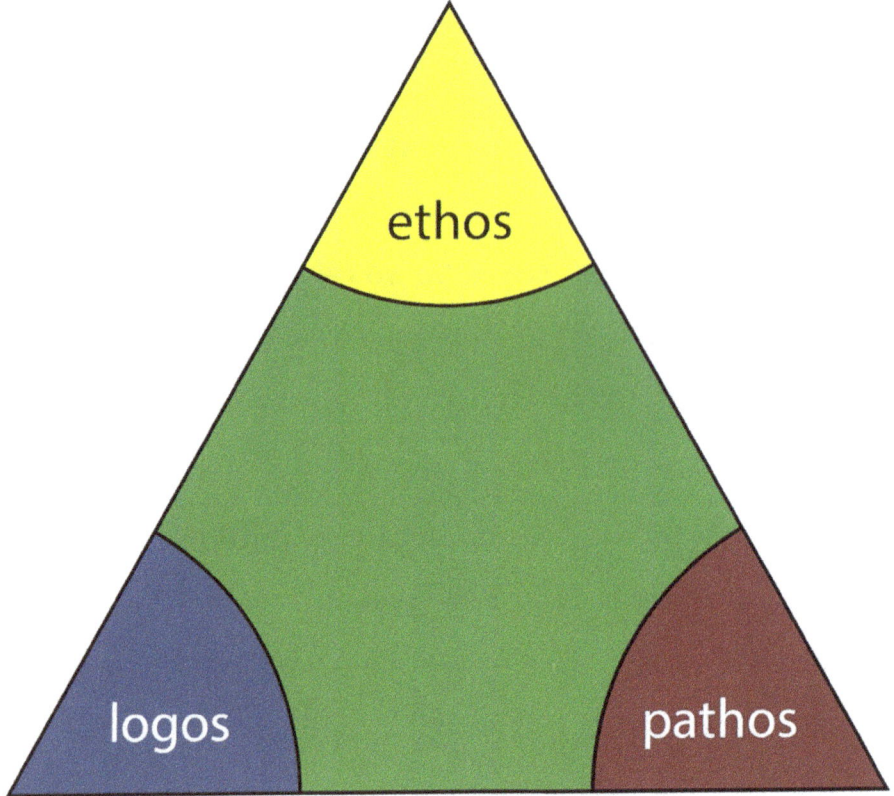
Figure 1: the rhetorical triangle

(The American elementary tradition of Show & Tell is a bright spot in the problematic K-12; note how many Americans are more articulate when speaking than when writing?)

It's also where technology can pay dividends. A kid wants to present using PowerPoint? Let them. Or incorporate a video? Terrific. A key advantage with our model is that kids get to choose their preferred modality across a range of problems to solve. (A paucity of allowed learning modes is a key problem with today's schooling.)

Once again, you learn best by teaching someone else.

That's speaking as a fourth skill, with the oral presentation its assessable outcome. Next up: **arithmetic**.

# Adding arithmetic

Arithmetic isn't the same as mathematics. (In fact, most mathematicians are poor at it.) It's an easy facility with the basic operations of real numbers: addition, subtraction, multiplication, division, exponentiation and extraction of roots, negative numbers, percentages, fractions and decimals.

The thinking skill arithmetic fosters is a sense of proportion: grasping "how big" things are and what happens when you act on them. This skill needs to bed into a child's mind, *deeply*. An instinct for how long 479BCE was before 1945; the ability to "size" a ton of metal or the distance to the sun—all put numbers in context in the mind. What matters is that worked examples from the real world are practiced over and over again, positioning numbers as the way we measure our world. Which means calculators still don't have a place.

(If Asian kids are good at maths, it's because they practice these basic operations throughout childhood, at speeds—if you've ever seen a Hong Kong cram school in session—that are truly startling.)

Again, arithmetic isn't a subject per se, but a core skill that connects and enables others.

Accordingly, the key tool of arithmetic is the **worked example**. A real world narrative of how numbers came together and their result. (Business schools use case studies for the same reason.)

# Learning logic

Finally, our sixth basic skill is one *never* taught in State schools, because it's the one most likely to foster questioning of authority: **logic**.

At its simplest, logic is a method for differentiating **what is** from **what is not**. It's an area of mathematics every bit as vital as arithmetic. To realise it's not taught routinely even in private schools is *shocking*. Because its tenets are simple and useful, even fun.

Formal logic is a set of inferences that follow from a proposition leading to a conclusion. (All men are mortal / Socrates is a man / Therefore, Socrates is mortal.) The crucial skill is to reduce an argument in written language—with all its linguistic flotsam and jetsam—to its logical form, so that form can be validated and the argument proven or disproven. (All A are B. C is an A. Therefore C is a B.) In other words, working with concepts rather than percepts.

By age 13, the logical operators ⊃, ⇔, and ≢ should be as familiar to a schoolchild as + and -.

Logic is a method for thinking critically, so like our other five, it cuts across all school subjects.

The key tool for this skill is the **formal proof**, the thinking-through of a worked example in writing. Writing formal proofs isn't something that has to wait until college years; kids as young as 6 show a surprising facility with them. Teaching logic as a core skill lets them shine.

$$R + W + L + S + A + L = \text{thinking}$$

So there you have it. Six skills for thinking come before all else: reading, writing, listening, speaking, arithmetic, and logic. Five of them any teacher can teach with both hands tied, the sixth easily added with a few CPD days.

But here's the really big change for our model:

When work is set, in any subject, a child can answer the assignment **however (s)he likes**.

Answer a maths problem with an essay. A book report with a video presentation. A history review with a spoken script.

Process is not mandated. Only *outcomes* matter.

Why? Because our model of education is to get kids

*thinking*. And people have different preferred modalities—natural preferences today's schools attempt to squish like bugs.

This is nonstandard, yes. It's a lot harder to mark than that monstrous pit of mediocrity, the multiple choice test. But that's the point. The people doing the marking are *teachers*. Their only goal is: *can this child practice what was taught?* To a skilled teacher, that answer is evident whatever modality it's delivered in.

Answers matter, but answer *formats* should not.

Letting a child submit coursework in the format he/she prefers lets them *choose their learning mode*. It also allows the creativity and freedom to make mistakes that turns school from a hellhole of rote memorisation to a true place of enlightenment.

(Mild hyperbole, but you get the principle.)

Some kids learn by constantly talking, integrating new concepts by exploring language. For them, a rhetorical defence is ideal. Some kids can't sit still, unable to work through problems without moving. For them, a video selfie might be their answer. While others are studious and introverted. They'll submit every assignment as an essay. All of which is fine.

The kid solves a problem the way he thinks he can solve it. The teacher bases their grade on how effectively the kid reasoned out the answer, whatever their learning mode.

It's an approach that takes no prisoners, requiring skilled judgement from the teacher. But equally it permits no place to hide for the pupil.

Sounds hard? Yes. But far more professionally fulfilling for the educator; she's engaging her intellect every time she lifts a red pen. Even better, it does away with the artificiality of exams altogether. Grade Point Averages, a far more real-world practice for ongoing assessment (a working life doesn't happen under exam conditions) are all that's needed to check progress over the years. No exams needed.

If these six basics percolate the entire curriculum of taught subjects—not as discrete skills, but as tools for thinking that stitch together everything else in the school day—an ability to think is the result.

RWLSAL is at the core of it all.

Yeah, lousy acronym.

# ... AND WHAT IT SHOULDN'T

A rule of business: *do what you're good at*. If you're not good at it, don't do it. (In economics, this is Riccardo's Law of Comparative Advantage, aka the "magic of trade" that maximises value for all.)

School is for teaching children to think. Nothing else. So—especially in schools funded by the taxpayer—let's limit their remit to just that.

Skilled as they are, teachers are *teachers*. Not social workers or surrogate parents. Nor should we ask them to be. Teaching is hard enough without endless mission creep.

That means no breakfast clubs or sports teams or school trips mandated by the powers that be. They're *luxuries*, up to the individual school.

There's no room in school for team sport, or music, or art, either. In fact, a major failing of State schools is they attention they place on these. They're fun, perhaps. But they're not core to education.

(And of *course* there's no Gender Studies, or Relationships, or Religious Stuff. A thinking person can understand other people without needing the tribalism of today's culture wars rammed down her throat. Because thinking is the action of an *individual*. And a thinking individual can see beyond the special interest group.)

To make this point, let's look at the prime deletable material.

## No sport.

American High Schools build baseball diamonds and football fields that cost hundreds of thousands of dollars, routinely spending more per student on sports than on any other subject. British ones allocate the same timetable resource to PE as to maths.

Yet 13m US kids are obese. UK children hold the No. 1 spot in Europe for Type II diabetes. If the goal of PE departments is to foster a lifelong love of physical exercise, they're failing dismally.

Yet sports, needing specialist equipment and facilities, skew the cost base for any school massively. Given their cost, you'd think they'd at least fulfil some basic criteria, like keeping kids fit.

But they don't. Indeed, they don't fulfil even the simplest criteria.

If kids want to kick a ball or score points for running around, great—that's what weekends are for. But as a school subject, sport should go out the window.

Along with any teacher who thinks otherwise.

**No art.**

Yes, art matters. It's one of the six branches of philosophy that underpin *everything*: aesthetics, the idea of beauty. (Along with metaphysics, epistemology, ethics, politics, and logic.)

But not the easel-and-brushes kind.

Like music, drawing and painting are abstract arts, with a language far more subjective and less useful for life than others. The need for aesthetics, in our curriculum, is answered by literature.

Let's leave daubing on paper for the years pre-6, who love to do it . . . and the ones after 16 who want to make it a career.

## No music.

The most useless of all subjects routinely taught in schools is music.

Like sport, it requires specialist equipment and facilities. Also like sport, it teaches a skill few will use later in life. (And even fewer will make a living from).

Worst of all, it makes a hell of a racket.

Music is to be enjoyed, not endured. Which means it's a hobby. And hobbies aren't for the school day.

No music on our curriculum.

**No computing.**

Really?

In a global economy driven by technology, school shouldn't include computer science?

No more than learning to drive should need an engine-building certificate.

The huge majority of people will use computers, but as a *tool*. Not as software developers. However well-meant, it's ridiculous to include such specific skills in a well-rounded curriculum.

Computing is a means to an end. Not a school subject.

# And no religion, too.

Sort of obvious, this one. But let's repeat: beliefs in the supernatural have no place in school.

(In private, at home? *That's* fine. For many, a religion provides comfort. But it's got nothing to do with thinking. In fact, it's the opposite.)

Our curriculum includes literature and history. Which, given religion's influence on the past, put religion where it belongs: in context. As a shaper and influencer. Not a subject in itself.

School is about what's real. Not what isn't.

## A MINIMALIST CURRICULUM

Beyond the six basics, a core three intertwined subject areas complete our well-rounded education that teaches thinking.

Yes, just *three*.

(Admittedly with tag-ons, because each main subject—mathematics, history, literature—acts as the stage for a vast array of choices.)

Added as extras are two subjects: languages (any one you like) and exercise (functional movement). But they're optional for schools.

It's a *simple* curriculum, developing an effortless understanding in the basics that enables everything else—all practical skills, all intellectual subjects, all physical development—to arise naturally, from the curiosity of the child him/herself. Each subject chosen for a critical purpose.

Let's look at each.

# Mathematics / STEM

Our model treats children's education as a training in concepts. Maths (separate to arithmetic) is core, because it's the most conceptual thing out there.

Mathematics, as a symbolic representation of reality, brings the entire universe within the scope of a scribbled page. Taught properly—in terms of interrelated concepts, not a disparate grab-bag of modules—it's not something to be feared: it is something wondrous, a facility for understanding *everything*.

Teaching conceptually, of course, means swinging in many examples from different areas, constantly demonstrating how they fit into a unified whole. So the subject isn't divided into "pure" and "applied": it's set in a context of STEM. Science, Technology, Engineering, *and* Mathematics. Algebra, geometry, trigonometry, and calculus are the theories and methods by which we understand nature, generalise its concepts, and turn it to our advantage—but each needs relating *to* nature to be comprehended by young minds, and STEM does the job.

The S is mostly physics, the science that underlies all others, although life sciences like evolution get a look-in. T is the illustrated outcome of doing S. While the E puts maths further into practical context: vectors and forces at work in statics and dynamics, the electromagnetic spectrum as radio and circuits.

With this contextual framework, mathematics to

age 16 can be much more ambitious than in a cluttered curriculum. As the basis of physics, there's no reason why advanced calculus and field equations should wait until college, for example.

As a purely conceptual and deductive subject, maths is at the core of thinking: it forces intellectual rigour and clarity of process like no other subject. It shows not how complex things are, but how fundamentally *simple*. The more maths kids get, the better they'll think throughout their lives.

Next to an equally canonical subject in our core curriculum: **history**.

# History / PPE

If maths is the nature of reality, history is the nature of humanity. (Indeed, it can act as the *whole* of "the humanities".) Studying history lets us understand our species by its actions—and perhaps not condemn ourselves to repeat them.

What's great about history is that it can teach conceptual notions of motivation and action at all scales, with a *wealth* of examples to illustrate it. It's a study of principles: the basic factors driving human existence, the role of ideas, and the effects of those ideas on different societies.

Looking at history's sweep can demonstrate which are "human nature", and which are fads and fashions.

Which means an individual school can use whatever examples and situations it wants, with the proviso it must teach conceptually and connectedly (sic) showing how each case fits in the broader story of human history. Which allows immense breadth for customisation. A country's place in the world. Or a culture's influence outside its borders. Or the impact of tools and techniques.

What's more, learning history enables an understanding of its more abstract and theoretical concepts rarely taught before college level: Philosophy, Politics, and Economics, or PPE. While essential to a deep understanding of the world, they're not teachable to fourteen-year-olds without a thick base layer to support them: that foundation is history.

Helpfully, studying history through its concepts rather than percepts also dispels "cultural relativism", the postmodern "idea" that all approaches to society are somehow equally worthy. History fosters a critical sense of *value judgements* in the child, of knowing how what's happening now fits into what happened before—and that what happened was not an accident.

(It's also easy to integrate with other subjects. History can be taught through the story of scientific discovery. Or of world exploration. Or of written works. Or . . . you get the idea.)

History, the study of humans, is the second of our three core subjects. Next up: **literature**.

## Literature / arts

Riffing again on the six branches of philosophy, maths is how we understand nature: a study of metaphysics and logic. History is how we understand humans, taking in ethics and politics. That leaves aesthetics and epistemology, musings on what it means to *be* human—answered by **art**, humanity's view of itself.

In our stripped-to-what-matters subject set, **literature** is the Chosen One for the arts. For a singular reason: it's the easiest to teach thinking with.

(By "literature", we mean studying novels, short stories, plays, and poetry for their ideas and the concepts they communicate. Not "English Language", which is part of RWLSAL.)

Most art is *perceptual*, principally appealing to the senses. Of all arts, literature is the most *conceptual*, using *language* to express its ideas. So literature, by far, is the best fit for our model's need for an aesthetic subject.

Again, it's up to the individual school what Great Books to teach, as long as they're taught conceptually. When the goal is to develop critical thinking and reasoning skills, it doesn't matter whether the actual book is the Illiad or the Ramayana. One criterion, though: the books (and plays, and poems) should be canonical. And we're not just talking Chaucer and Shakespeare here.

(Side note: school's obsession with Shakespeare has

been putting young people off literature for centuries. Yes, the Bard puts on a good show, but consider how odd it is that 14-year-olds reading stage directions by a 16$^{th}$-century actor is seen as non-negotiable.)

Every culture has its canonical texts, and there are benefits both in teaching a narrow-but-deep list dominated by dead white males, and a world-girdling list spanning Gilgamesh to Dostoevsky. As long as it connects in coherent context to other taught subjects, it's the school's, and by definition the parents', choice. But both lists share one trait: there's probably not much *new* stuff on there.

That's literature, the third of three core subjects on our curriculum. Now for the two optionals.

## (Languages)

The poetic beauty of French and Spanish. The intricate ideograms of traditional Chinese. The exotic simplicity of Indonesian, getting Malaysian as a bonus.

It'd be a shame to leave languages out of school, wouldn't it?

The good news: with such a drastically reduced curriculum, many schools will have room for some extras. One would be a **language**.

*Which* language doesn't matter. Communicating in another tongue lets you step inside the mind of someone with a different culture and history—a great addendum for thinking.

So if a school wants to offer a language and can teach and assess it in the same way as other subjects— nothing should stop them.

## (Exercise)

Same with exercise. Sport doesn't teach thinking, so it's no part of our model. But the Greek ideal of *mens sana in corpore sano*—a healthy mind in a healthy body—is important. A body is your machine for doing thinking in.

We owe it to tomorrow's adults to at least introduce a way to take care of it.

So in our model there's an option for schools to consider simple and effective exercise programmes that foster health and strength—ideally movement-and-skill-based, like the calisthenics ("beautiful strength") that dates back to ancient Greece. Following the same principles as all other teaching:

you're not teaching *what*, but *how*. *This* is how to maintain lifelong good posture in a world of hunched shoulders. *This* is the way to keep your core up to scratch and avoid pain later on. As with all subjects, there's a reading and writing element too: impart *understanding* of the body, not just put them through an hour's torture every Wednesday.

Exercise, of course, has nothing to do with bats and balls. Leave that for weekends.

# A NEW FUNDING MODEL

So that's our core curriculum: an early focus on reading, writing, listening, speaking, arithmetic, and logic, with history, mathematics, and literature as the main subjects. Notice anything about how all of these can be meaningfully taught?

They're *cheap*.

With limited time to inculcate abilities in the most impressionable decade of life, school should concentrate on the essentials. So *all* our skills and subjects can be taught without equipment or specialised facilities. At a pinch, none needs more than a room and pencils.

(Because the *teacher* is the only factor that matters,

remember?)

Yet the UK spends £6,300 a year per pupil on a secondary education system with harassed teachers, rancorous parents, and class sizes of 22-27. That's not much less per head than many *private* schools, but the private school will have class sizes below 16, more engaged pupils, and better-paid teachers.

It gets worse. Each pupil, even in a generous 36-week State school year, is in class for just 720 hours for that £6,300. That's a £236 cost per 27-pupil class.

Ask business consultants whether they'd train people for £236/hr and you'll be *inundated* with Yeses. (It's a fee comparable to top consultants and lawyers.) And that £236 isn't a one-off sale: it's a recurring, virtually guaranteed revenue stream.

So let's look at school funding from a different—and more businesslike—perspective. A pupil isn't a snot-nosed bundle of scruffiness, but *a £60,000+ recurring revenue item in a ten-year engagement.*

And a school can have hundreds of them.

This figure alone justifies our high salaries for teachers: a sensible maximum class size (say 25) means an annual gross of £157,500 from a single teacher if they deliver a world-class service. And it doesn't stop there—if you change perspective away from boxes ticked and towards *value created.*

This is easily justified by business case. Let's treat an educated child—the 16-year-old leaving school able to think—as the asset to the economy he or she will become.

An ability to think supercharges your lifetime earnings potential. In our model, the proportion of 16-year-olds leaving school capable of thinking triples, at minimum. Let's be equally conservative with the lifetime earnings guesstimate, and set it at half that earned by a graduate: a time-discounted £250,000.

A rough back-of-envelope for this UK model: if that increases the number of people adding value at that level by 200% from its current 885,000, that's not far off a *£450 billion* shot in the arm for the economy. Around a quarter of GDP.

Compare that payback to what the UK currently spends on primary and secondary education: £72bn. And with education cumulative, that's really only the start of it.

So with a proper business model behind it, the case for increasing primary and secondary education funding gets easier. And, of course, the minimalist education this model proposes is cheaper to deliver, with no requirement for playing fields, auditoriums, or cafeterias.

(Of course, if a school *wants* to invest—in an starchitect-designed building, or innovative teaching facilities—it's welcome to do so. Government in this model proscribes outcomes, not methods.)

Which means our £53,000 teaching salary starts looking like excellent value.

But it doesn't end there. Schools today are specialised buildings—but market forces may lead to much smaller schools. And smaller schools are easier to house. Perhaps a future school might have fewer than 100 pupils and a half-dozen teachers, each focussed on delivering outcomes.

Let's look at such an approach.

# A PRIVATE APPROACH FOR STATE SCHOOLS

Almost any private school is a better place to put your child than almost any State school.

This isn't the State school's fault; many teachers are dedicated and hardworking. It's the State *sector*'s fault. Distorted incentives create, well, distortions.

But it's not either/or. Note that in the UK's State system—academies, grammars—the closer the model is to the private system, the better the school.

So let's be blunt here:

All schools should be like private schools. Investing in their own resources, delivering services in competition with other schools, succeeding or failing on whether they satisfy customers.

That's the "System of the World", free-market capitalism, that leads to prosperity and value in every place that follows it and misery and poverty everywhere that doesn't.

Looked at this way, a 1,000-pupil comprehensive is a £6.3m business producing a longterm return on investment. At market rate, a business worth £8-10m or so—and a lot more if you look at the returns to GDP instead of the school alone.

So what if we gave those businesses to the people who make them valuable—the teachers?

(Just as another book, "How to do Healthcare", gave hospitals to the people who work in them.)

The essence of attracting great people is to offer rewards that recognise their contribution. How about shares in the business they'll work for, with the prospect of excellent returns if they produce the outcomes they're charged with?

Just a thought.

## VALIDATING VOUCHERS

Of course, the attraction of State school is that parents without the cash don't have to pay for it. (Not directly, anyway.)

So in the absence of a totally private system (which would be the ideal) let's take the government budget and put it where it matters most: with the parents.

Before your child turns 6, you the parent get a voucher for the first year of your child's education. Then another, every year. You can spend it at any school that'll take your child. Anywhere.

It might not cover the whole amount. We're in a free market, so the school can charge whatever it wants on top. (Whether it gets it, with open competition, is another matter.) Perhaps some schools, mindful of their public mission, will keep their fees equal to the voucher. (They'll be oversubscribed if they're good.) Perhaps other schools, new and anxious to establish a reputation, will charge *less*. And parents will make their choices.

This basic approach has been successful even with limited application. Britain's Academies—which have to attract pupils in a different way to typical State schools—are often highly rated, despite being sited in some of the UK's most deprived areas. While the USA's Magnet and (later) Charter schools show equally encouraging results.

So anyone who thinks a free-market system means poor families will be shut out doesn't understand how markets work.

If their schools succeed, there's a huge incentive for a team of expert teachers to expand their market, by setting up another. Perhaps taking over a failing one. (There'll be plenty of choice.) And parents can move their child freely between schools, with none of that "catchment area" nonsense. (The best markets are borderless.)

This aligns incentives between teacher, school, and parents. And resolves—in a puff of logic—common teachers' complaints about pay-by-results. Why should any teacher oppose merit pay—getting paid more for doing a great job—if they can see how it benefits them as individuals? That's the basis of essentially all *private* enterprise.

(Some teachers may scoff that different schools won't be comparable; that kids all come from different backgrounds and abilities. Well, grow up, Sir. Customers do too, and they're paying their *own* money.)

Imagine a world with no essential difference between private and State schools. Where strengths and specialisations differ, but everyone's working for their customers not the government, and parents exercise choice based on who they most want to spend money with. Good schools become great ones; bad schools either improve or get taken off the table.

That's a world worth thinking about.

## DRRIIIING!

School's out. And so, now, is this little idea about teaching kids what really matters: to think.

Of course, there'll be opposition. When change is presented to an entrenched clique, there always is. So if you're a teacher, all I ask is that you give some thought to how much *fun* it might be.

In this model, your world *will* be rocked. Your skills *will* be stretched. You *will* end the week stooped, flushed, and ready to drain a bottle of Malbec in fifteen minutes or less.

But how is that different to today?

And instead of that exhaustion coming from frustration and red tape, it'll come from exercising your real talents. Understanding kids as individuals, assessing their work according to their preferred learning styles, choosing how and even what you teach, as long as it contributes to an agreed outcome.

You've got freedom to do what you're best at, Sir. At last.

Just give it a thought, will you?

# ABOUT CHRIS

Chris Worth is a London-based copywriter and author of the guide to effective freelancing **100 Days, 100 Grand**. Google it or head for 100days100grand.com.

At work, he creates campaigns and content backed by meaningful insights, mostly for technology clients. (He does the research and analysis too, btw—his USP.)

Interests include adventure travel and extreme sports. He's lived in six countries, visited 60, and is a qualified sky and scuba diver with a passion for calisthenics and kettlebells. But he's never without his Kindle. See him at chrisdoescontent.com.

www.ingramcontent.com/pod-product-compliance
Lightning Source LLC
Chambersburg PA
CBHW080626030426
42336CB00018B/3092